MAKING THINGS FLOAT & SINK

© Aladdin Books Ltd 1995
Created and produced by
NW Books, 28 Percy Street
London W1P OLD

First published in the United States in 1995 by
Copper Beech Books, an imprint of
The Millbrook Press, 2 Old New Milford Road
Brookfield, Connecticut 06804

Editor:
Susannah Le Besque

Design:
David West Children's Book Design
Illustrator:
Tony Kenyon
Photography:
Roger Vlitos
Consultant:
Dr. Bryson Gore

*The publishers wish to point out
that all the photographs reproduced
in this book have been posed by models.*

Library of Congress Cataloging-in-Publication Data
Gibson, Gary, 1957-
Making things float and sink / by Gary Gibson :
illustrated by Tony Kenyon. p. cm. -- (Science for fun)
Includes index.
ISBN 1-56294-617-X (lib. bdg.)
ISBN 1-56294-635-8 (pbk.)
1. Archimedes' principle--Juvenile literature.
2. Floating bodies--Experiments--Juvenile
literature. [1. Water--Experiments. 2.
FLoating bodies--Experiments. 3.
Experiments] I. Kenyon, Tony, ill. II.
Title. III. Series: Gibson, Gary. 1957-
Science for fun
QC147.5.G53   1995   94-41189
532'.02--dc20   CIP AC

SCIENCE
FOR FUN

MAKING THINGS
FLOAT & SINK

GARY GIBSON

COPPER BEECH BOOKS
Brookfield, Connecticut

CONTENTS

INTRODUCTION

For thousands of years people have
built boats to sail on the rivers
and seas. Since then we have
been fascinated by things that float
and sink. Why does a giant steel ship
float, yet a single steel screw sinks? Why
does ice float on water? How does a submarine both
float *and* sink? This book contains a selection of
exciting "hands-on" projects to help answer some
of these questions.

Whenever this
symbol appears
adult supervision is
required.

GET AN
ADULT
TO DO THIS
FOR YOU

WHY DO THINGS FLOAT?

Wood, cork and ice all float no matter what size or shape they are. However, materials such as modeling clay or steel, sometimes float and sometimes sink. With these materials, it is their shape that decides whether they float or sink.

MAKE A CLAY BOAT

1 Fill a large plastic bowl with water from the tap.

2 Try to float a lump of modeling clay on the surface of the water. Try floating marbles too. Watch them sink.

3 Using your thumbs, press the clay into a boat shape. Hollow out the inside.

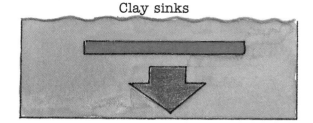

4 Draw a sailor on a sheet of cardboard. Color him in and cut out. Fold along the dotted lines as shown so he can sit up.

Clay sinks

Clay and air float

5 Sit the sailor in the boat. Now float the boat on the water. Put a marble in your boat. It will sink slightly but remains upright.

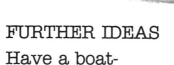

WHY IT WORKS

One ounce of water takes up more space than one ounce of clay. Because clay is denser than water it sinks. Shaped into a boat, clay fills with air. Air and clay together are less dense than water, so the boat floats.

FURTHER IDEAS
Have a boat-building competition with some friends. Each make a boat using the same amount of clay. Whose boat can hold the most marbles?

ICEBERG AHOY!

When most liquids freeze to solids they become more dense. Water is different. When water freezes it expands (causing burst pipes in winter) and becomes less dense. Ice floats because it is less dense than water.

Giant blocks of ice floating in the sea are called icebergs. Ships must take care to avoid icebergs.

WATCH AN ICE-CUBE MELT

1 Add some food coloring to a jar of water. Add enough coloring to turn the water a bright color.

2 Pour the colored water into an ice-cube tray. Put it in a freezer overnight.

3 Fill up a large container with hot tap water. Ask an adult to help you.

5 As the ice becomes water, the color moves around in the warmer water. It sinks to the bottom of the container.

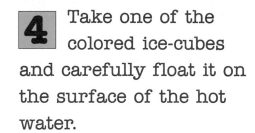

4 Take one of the colored ice-cubes and carefully float it on the surface of the hot water.

WHY IT WORKS

As the ice melts to water its density increases. This makes it sink to the bottom of the container. There it mixes with the water in the jar and warms up. It becomes less dense and moves back toward the surface.

Melted ice

FURTHER IDEAS Make a volcano. Fill a jar with hot water. Add coloring. Cover the top of the jar with paper held in place with a rubber band. Put the jar in a bowl of cold water. Pierce the paper. Watch the volcano erupt.

COLORFUL PAPER

It is not only boats and icebergs that float on water. Oil-based liquids that are less dense than water also float on top of water. We sometimes see escaped crude oil floating on the sea in a thin layer that stretches for miles. Such oil slicks can harm the seabed, fish, and birds.

MAKE COLORED PAPER

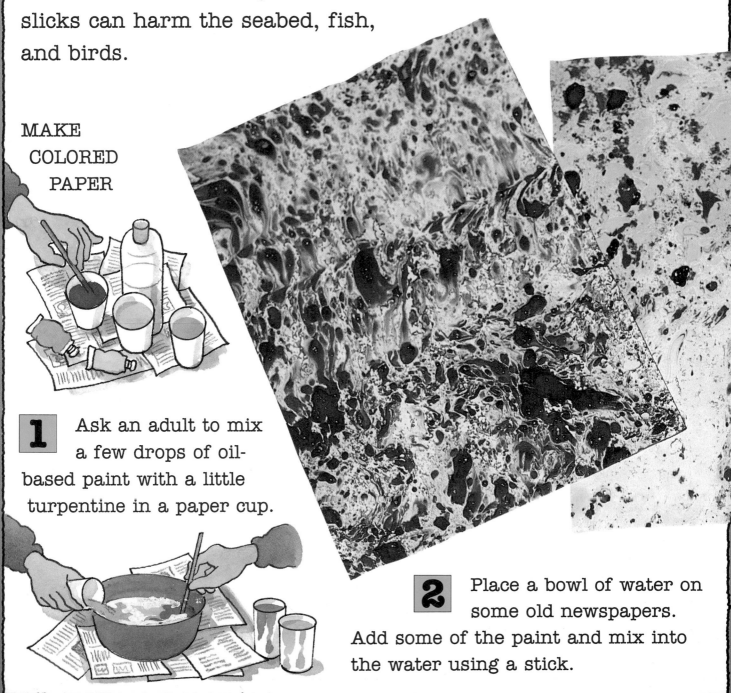

1 Ask an adult to mix a few drops of oil-based paint with a little turpentine in a paper cup.

2 Place a bowl of water on some old newspapers. Add some of the paint and mix into the water using a stick.

3 Carefully lower a sheet of plain paper onto the surface of the water. Let the paper soak up the paint.

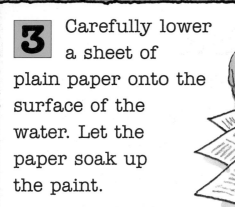

WHY IT WORKS

Oil paints are less dense than water so they float on the surface. For this reason salad oil floats on top of vinegar. You can make the separate layers mix together by shaking them hard.

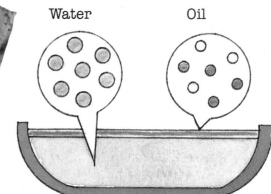

Water   Oil

4 Remove the paper and leave it to dry. Repeat using fresh paper. Stir the water to get different patterns.

FURTHER IDEAS
Try making different patterns by changing the colors of paint. Let the papers dry. Use your favorite patterns for writing paper.

FLOATING LIQUIDS

Many liquids are like water and mix easily with it. But some liquids do not mix with water unless they are forced to. Oils and syrups do not mix well with water. Some liquids are less dense and float on top of water (see pages 10-11). Others are denser so water floats on top of them.

MAKE LAYERS OF FLOATING LIQUIDS

GET AN ADULT TO DO THIS FOR YOU

1 Find a clean, empty plastic soda bottle. Ask an adult to cut the top off with a sharp knife.

2 Slowly pour in some syrup so there is a 3/4 of an inch layer in the bottom. Let the syrup settle.

3 Next slowly pour 3/4 of an inch of cooking oil over the layer of syrup.

4 Finally, carefully pour in about 3/4 of an inch of water.

12

5 Examine the three layers. They float on top of each other without mixing. See what happens if you stir gently with a spoon.

WHY IT WORKS

The layers of liquid refuse to mix with each other. The syrup is at the bottom because it is the densest. The oil is the least dense of the three and so floats on the very top.

FURTHER IDEAS
Try floating different objects on your layers of liquid. Experiment with things that you would expect to sink in water.

FLOATING EGGS

How can you tell whether an egg is good or bad without breaking it? Fresh eggs sink if placed in a bowl of fresh water because they are denser than water. But if an egg turns bad, it floats in water. This is because the yolk and white have dried up, which makes it less dense than a good egg.

MAKE AN EGG FLOAT

GET AN ADULT TO DO THIS FOR YOU

1 Find two large containers. Fill one with hot tap water and the other with cold tap water. Get an adult to help.

2 Add a spoonful of table salt to the hot water. Stir in the salt until it has all dissolved.

3 Put a fresh egg into the salty water to see if it floats. If it doesn't, add more salt until it does.

Salt dissolved in water increases the density of water. Denser liquids are better at keeping objects afloat.

This is why many things that sink in fresh water will float in salted water.

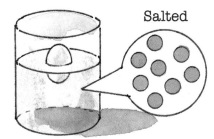

Salted

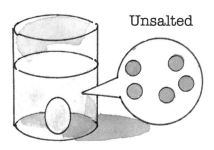

Unsalted

4 You cannot float the egg in fresh water but in salty water the same egg floats. Challenge your friends to explain it!

FURTHER IDEAS

See how long it takes for a fresh egg to go bad when not refrigerated. Test it in a bowl of fresh water each day. Dispose of the bad egg *carefully* when you've finished.

DIFFERENT DEPTHS

We have seen that each liquid has its own particular density. The denser or "heavier" the liquid, the better it is at making things float in it. Brewers of beer need to know the exact density of beer to ensure the beer tastes just right. A hydrometer is used to test its density.

MAKE A HYDROMETER

1 Pour equal amounts of syrup, cooking oil and hot water into three containers of the same size.

2 Cut a plastic drinking straw into three equal lengths. Each will make a hydrometer.

3 Make three small balls out of clay. Attach one to the end of each straw.

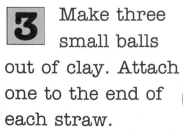

FURTHER IDEAS

Float your hydrometer in a bowl of water. Add salt or sugar to the water. What effect does this have on the hydrometer?

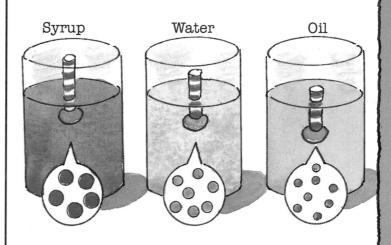

Syrup   Water   Oil

4 Carefully place each hydrometer into the liquids. Compare the different levels at which the hydrometers float.

The particles of dense liquids are bigger or closer together. Dense liquids push harder on the hydrometer. The harder the push, the higher up in the liquid the hydrometer floats.

UNSINKABLE

Boats and ships are always built to be as stable as possible. This means that they do not get pushed over easily by waves in rough seas. Most boats and ships capsize and sink if they are pushed too far. A buoy is a channel marker. Because it is there to warn of danger, it is vital that it never gets pushed over.

MAKE A BUOY

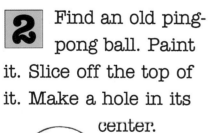

1 Half fill a large container with water.

GET AN ADULT TO DO THIS FOR YOU

2 Find an old ping-pong ball. Paint it. Slice off the top of it. Make a hole in its center.

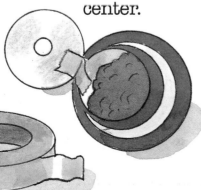

3 Fill the inside of the buoy with clay and tape the top back on.

4 Make a flag out of a triangle of paper and a drinking straw.

5 Stick the flag into the hole in the top of the buoy.

6 Put the buoy in the water. Make some waves. See how difficult it is to push the buoy over.

WHY IT WORKS

The clay acts as "ballast." Ballast is spare weight. The ballast pulls downward into the water and keeps the buoy upright. Boats carry ballast to keep them stable at sea.

FURTHER IDEAS Compare the stability of your buoy with the boat you made in Project 1. Waves lapping over the side of the boat can easily cause it to capsize.

PORT AND STARBOARD

You may have noticed that ships and large boats have steering wheels. Smaller boats have a tiller instead. Both wheel and tiller are used to control a "rudder." The rudder is used to steer the boat.

At sea, sailors say "port" for left and "starboard" for right.

GET AN ADULT TO HELP YOU WITH THIS

MAKE A BOAT WITH A RUDDER

1 Ask an adult to cut a boat shape from a piece of styrofoam. Make two holes as shown.

2 Make a brightly colored sail out of thin paper. Push a wooden stick through the sail.

3 Push the stick into the hole at the pointed end of the boat. Hold in place with clay.

4 Cut a rudder out of a waterproof milk carton. Tape it to a drinking straw.

Cocktail sticks

Rudder

5 Push the straw through the other hole. Hold the straw in place by pushing two cut-off cocktail sticks through it.

6 Launch the boat, blow into the sail and steer by turning the rudder.

WHY IT WORKS

1   2   3

If the rudder points in line with the flow of water (2) the boat moves straight on. If the rudder points to the left or right (1, 3), the flow of water is slowed by it and so the boat changes direction.

FURTHER IDEAS
Try to adjust the rudder of your boat so that the boat sails around in a circle when you blow into the sail.

JET POWER

Most boats and ships have propellers which push them along. The propeller cuts through the water, pushing it back behind the vessel. This push against the water "propels" or makes the vessel move forward. A jet-propelled boat can travel at high speeds without a propeller. The "jet" or fast-moving flow of water pushes the boat along.

MAKE A JET BOAT

1 Decorate an old plastic soda bottle. Weight the bottom of the bottle with clay.

2 Ask an adult to make a hole near the bottom of the bottle (right).

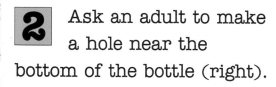

3 Place a balloon inside the bottle. Make sure you do not drop the balloon.

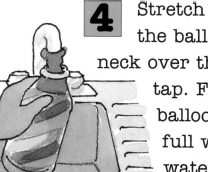

4 Stretch the balloon neck over the tap. Fill the balloon half full with water.

5 Pinch the balloon neck closed. Put clay around the bottle neck to weight the bottle.

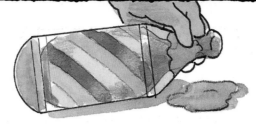

6 Still holding the end of the balloon, put the bottle in the bath.

7 Let go of the balloon. Watch the jet of water shoot out and push the boat along.

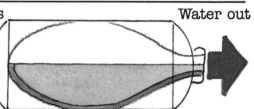

WHY IT WORKS

Boat moves forward

Water out

When the water shoots out of the balloon, it pushes against the water in the bath. This pushing force propels the jet boat forward. The quicker the water escapes from the balloon, the faster the boat travels.

FURTHER IDEAS
Cut a boat shape out of cardboard. Make a hole near the stern of the boat. Cut from the stern of the boat to the hole. Float the boat. Drop liquid soap in the hole. The boat will shoot forward.

DIVE DEEP!

Deep under the oceans are some of the last unexplored places on Earth. Deep-sea divers use vessels which can sink to the bottom and then float back to the surface again. Some marine animals such as jellyfish are also able to dive to great depths, then surface again.

MAKE A DIVING JELLYFISH

1 Find a large, clean plastic soda bottle. Fill it up to the top with tap water.

2 Cut both ends off a flexible plastic drinking straw to make a "U" shape.

3 Unbend a paper clip. Bend it into shape (shown at right). Push it into the ends of the straw.

4 Roll out three thin strips of clay. Loop them around the paper clip.

5 This is your jellyfish. Drop it into the bottle and screw the top back on. To make the jellyfish dive, squeeze the bottle.

WHY IT WORKS

When you squeeze the bottle, water is pushed into the straw, compressing the air. Water weighs more than air so the jellyfish gets heavier and sinks.

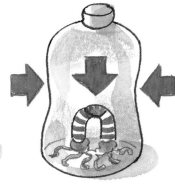

FURTHER IDEAS
Try making a diver from a small eye-dropper. Fill the dropper almost to the top with water then put it into the bottle of water.

FLOATING UNDERWATER

Submarines are special floating vessels because they can sink and then return to the surface. Ballast tanks control how deep they dive. To make the submarine sink, the tanks are filled with water. To make the submarine rise, the water is pumped out and replaced with air.

FLOATING UNDERWATER

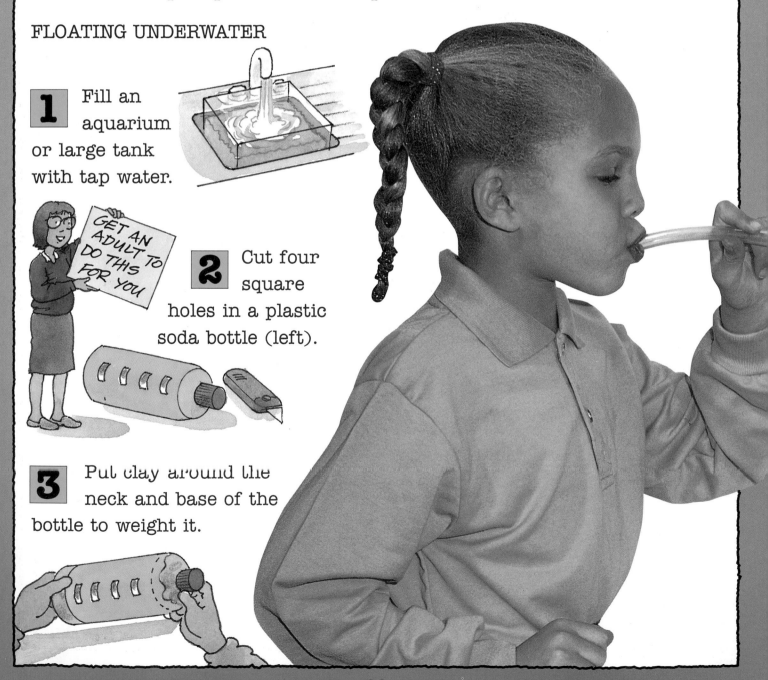

1 Fill an aquarium or large tank with tap water.

GET AN ADULT TO DO THIS FOR YOU

2 Cut four square holes in a plastic soda bottle (left).

3 Put clay around the neck and base of the bottle to weight it.

4 On the other side of the bottle make three holes. Make one large enough to fit a plastic tube.

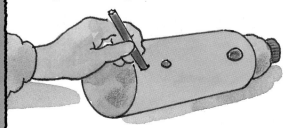

5 Decorate your submarine. Push the end of the tube into the larger of the three holes.

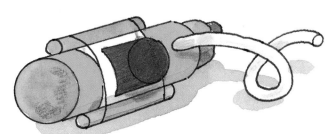

6 Try out your submarine. It will fill with water and sink. Blow into the tube to make it rise.

WHY IT WORKS

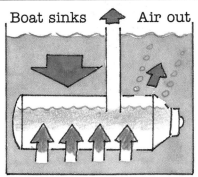

The submarine sinks when it fills with water (ballast). When you blow into the tube, the water is forced out and replaced by the air. Air is less dense than water so the submarine surfaces.

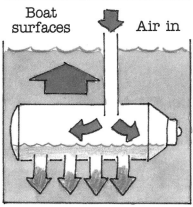

Boat sinks   Air out

Boat surfaces   Air in

FURTHER IDEAS
Put an empty bottle in the bottom of your aquarium. Let it fill with water. Now blow air into it with a straw to make the bottle rise.

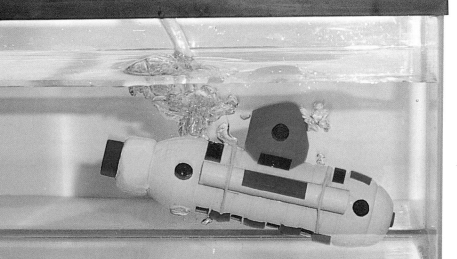

FLOATING ON AIR

The hovercraft is one of the great inventions of the twentieth century. It can travel on water or on land. The engines suck in air and then pump it downward. This creates a cushion of air that keeps the hovercraft from touching the surface over which it is traveling. The passengers enjoy a smooth and bump-free journey.

GET AN ADULT TO DO THIS FOR YOU

MAKE A HOVERCRAFT

1 Ask an adult to cut the top off a plastic soda bottle for you.

2 Wrap some clay around the base of the cut-off bottle top.

3 Make a skirt of paper to go around the clay. Make sure it hangs over it.

4 Blow up a balloon. Pinch the end. Carefully wrap the balloon around the bottle neck without letting it deflate.

5 Find a smooth surface. Place the hovercraft on it and let go of the balloon. Watch your hovercraft glide along.

WHY IT WORKS

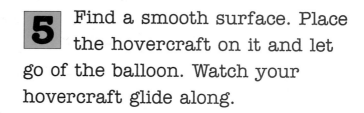

Air   Air

Air from the balloon escapes into the bottle top. The air pressure builds up until it creates a cushion that lifts the bottle slightly. It is the downward force of air that makes the hovercraft hover.

FURTHER IDEAS

Cut a hole in the bottom of a plastic margarine tub. Turn it upside down and fill it with air from a hairdrier. Watch it hover. Fill a paper bag with hot air from a hairdrier. What happens?

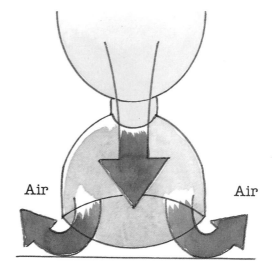

FANTASTIC FLOATING FACTS

Did you know that Aborigines are thought to have crossed from New Guinea to Australia in double canoes as long ago as 55,000 BC?

The *Titanic*, built in 1912, was claimed to be the unsinkable ocean liner. Tragically, on her first voyage across the Atlantic she hit an iceberg and sank. More than 1,500 of the 2,200 people on board lost their lives.

The marine jet engine was invented by a New Zealand engineer called William Hamilton in 1955. He tested his first jet boat in the fast-flowing rivers of New Zealand's South Island.

The first ocean liner ever to be made out of iron and driven by a propeller was the *Great Britain*. Designed by engineering genius, Isambard Kingdom Brunel, the *Great Britain* embarked on her first voyage in 1845.

The deepest dive by a submarine was made by the US Navy's deep submergence vessel, *Sea Cliff*, in March 1985. It reached the incredible depth of 20,000 feet.

The largest aircraft carriers in the world belong to the United States Navy. The USS *Nimitz* weighs more than 90,000 tons, is 1,092 feet long, 252 feet wide, and can carry 90 aircraft and a crew of about 5,700.

Plimsoll lines are marks on the side of a ship which indicate how much cargo can safely be loaded. Plimsoll lines show how low a vessel is lying in the water. The name comes from Samuel Plimsoll, who, in the nineteenth century, fought for safer working conditions for merchant sailors.

The first ever submarine was built by a Dutchman called Cornelis Jacobszoon Drebbel in 1620. It was made out of wood and was propelled by using oars.

GLOSSARY

BALLAST

Extra weight carried by vessels. It can be solid or liquid. Ballast helps keep a boat stable. When pumped out, it helps increase buoyancy.

COMPRESS

Squeeze together into less space.

BUOYANCY

The ability of a substance to float. Buoyancy depends on the density of the object.

DENSITY

The weight or heaviness of an object when it takes up a given amount of space.

FORCE

A push or a pull that makes an object change direction.

HYDROMETER

Instrument used to measure the density of a liquid by how deeply it sinks into the liquid.

JET

A fast-moving flow of water or air forced through a small outlet.

PORT

The left side of a boat or ship as you look forward.

PRESSURE

The force which presses down on a given area.

PROPELLER

A rotating object with spiral arms used to drive a boat or other vessel forward.

RUDDER

A flat steering object found under the stern of and underneath a boat.

STABLE

Steady; not easy to push over.

STARBOARD

The right side of a boat or ship as you look forward.

TILLER

The handle used to turn a rudder.

VOLUME

The amount of space something takes up.

INDEX